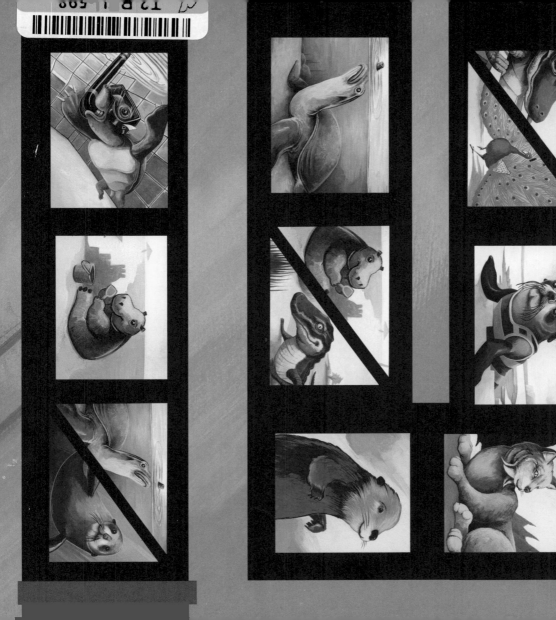

Have You Ever Seen a Hippo with Sunscreen?

Written by Etta Kaner · Illustrated by Jeff Szuc

Kids Can Press

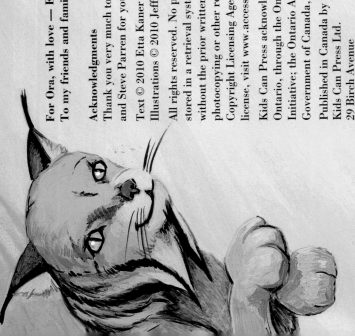

For Ora, with love — E.K.
To my friends and family for their unending support — J.S.

Acknowledgments
Thank you very much to Sharon T. Brown, Thea M. Edwards, Jim Helkie and Steve Parren for your time and expertise.

Kids Can Press acknowledges the financial support of the Government of Ontario, through the Ontario Media Development Corporation's Ontario Book Initiative; the Ontario Arts Council; the Canada Council for the Arts; and the Government of Canada, through the BPIDP, for our publishing activity.

Published in Canada by
Kids Can Press Ltd.
29 Birch Avenue
Toronto, ON M4V 1E2

www.kidscanpress.com

Published in the U.S. by
Kids Can Press Ltd.
2250 Military Road
Tonawanda, NY 14150

The artwork in this book was rendered in acrylic.
The text is set in Bodoni.

Edited by Karen Li and Samantha Swenson
Designed by Marie Bartholomew

This book is smyth sewn casebound.

Manufactured in Buji, Shenzhen, China, in 4/2010 by WKT Company

CM 10 0 9 8 7 6 5 4 3 2 1

Library and Archives Canada Cataloguing in Publication

Kaner, Etta
     Have you ever seen a hippo with sunscreen? / written by Etta Kaner ; illustrated by Jeff Szuc.

(Have you ever seen)
Interest age level: Ages 4–7.
ISBN 978-1-55453-337-4

1. Animals — Adaptation — Juvenile literature. I. Szuc, Jeff II. Title.
III. Series: Kaner, Etta. Have you ever seen.

QL49.K3625 2010   j591.4   C2010-900174-5

Kids Can Press is a Ⓛ Entertainment company

Contents

Have you ever seen a hippo with sunscreen?

That's silly.

I use sunscreen to protect
my skin from the sun.

Hippos don't use sunscreen.
People do.

6

What do hippos do?

Hippos make their own sunscreen. They ooze a sticky sweat that protects their skin from sunburn. The sweat also keeps hippos cool and stops germs from growing on their skin. As it dries, the sweat changes color — from clear to reddish brown. Amazing!

Have you ever ever seen
a beaver with a comb?

8

That's silly.

Beavers don't use combs.
People do.

I use a comb to untangle my hair.

10

What do beavers do?

Beavers comb their fur with their claws. They have two split claws on each of their hind feet. They use these claws to untangle their fur. They also use their front claws to comb out dirt, twigs and insects.

11

Have you ever seen
a turtle with a snorkel?

12

That's silly.

Turtles don't use snorkels.

People do.

I use a snorkel to breathe underwater.

14

What do turtles do?

Some softshell turtles float below the surface of the water. They stick their long noses out of the water to breathe. Other softshell turtles lie at the bottom of a shallow pond, waiting for a meal. They stretch their necks to reach their noses to the surface of the water.

15

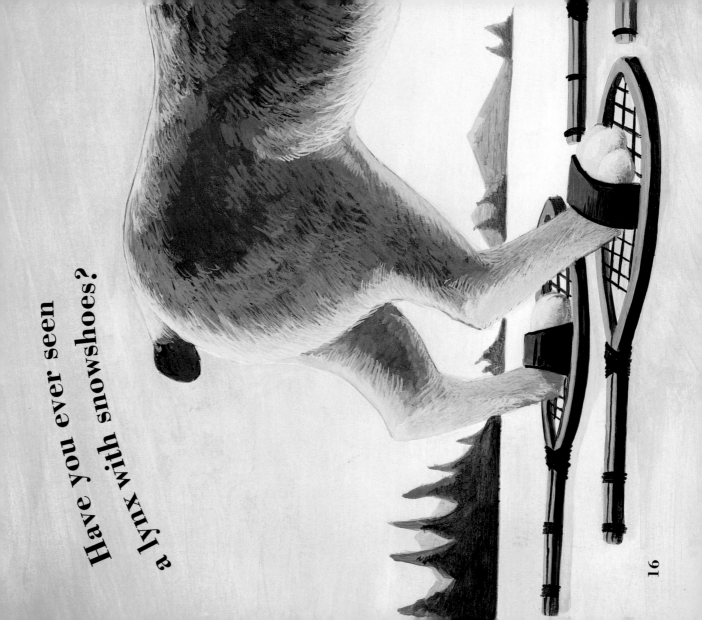

Have you ever ever seen
a lynx with snowshoes?

16

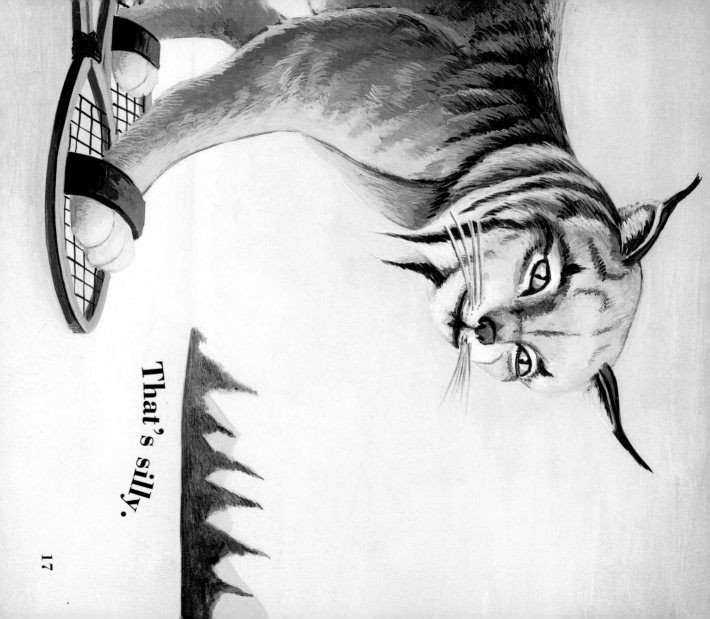

That's silly.

Lynx don't wear snowshoes.

People do.

I wear snowshoes to walk
in deep snow.

18

What do lynx do?

Lynx have big paws compared to the size of their bodies — it's like you wearing men's shoes. Each paw covers a large area of snow. That much snow can hold up the lynx's weight, so the lynx doesn't sink in.

Have you ever ever seen
an alligator with sunglasses?

That's silly.

Alligators don't wear sunglasses.
People do.

I wear sunglasses to shade
my eyes from the sun.

What do alligators do?

Alligators need to shade their eyes from the sun, too. Their eyes have long slits, or pupils, that let in light. In the sun, the pupils narrow to block out most of the sunlight. A cat's eyes work the same way.

Have you ever seen a peacock with jewelry?

24

Peacocks don't wear jewelry.
People do.

I wear jewelry to look beautiful.

What do peacocks do?

Male peacocks try to look beautiful for female peahens. They fan out their tail feathers to show off their colors. They puff up their side feathers to look bigger, and they dance. They do all this to say, "Choose me. I am the most beautiful of all."

27

28

Have you ever seen
a seal with nose plugs?

That's silly.

29

Seals don't wear nose plugs. People do.

I use nose plugs to keep water out of my nose.

What do seals do?

Seals have muscles that close their noses. They close their noses while looking for food underwater. They also close them while napping in the sea. When seals come up for air, they push open their nostrils to breathe.

31

Play Animal Games!

Have you ever seen an animal play a board game? Probably not. But you can play it! Just grab some friends and get started.

You will need

- 1 die
- 1 counter for each player (use buttons or coins)
- the game board inside the book covers, or make a photocopy

1. Players put their counters on the arrow. The first player rolls the die and moves the number of squares shown on the die.

2. If she lands on a square with one animal, the player must say two ways in which that animal is like a person or different from a person.

If there are two animals on a square, the player must say two ways in which the animals are alike or different from each other.

3. If the player can't give two comparisons, she loses her next turn.

4. Players take turns. The first player to reach the end wins. Good luck!

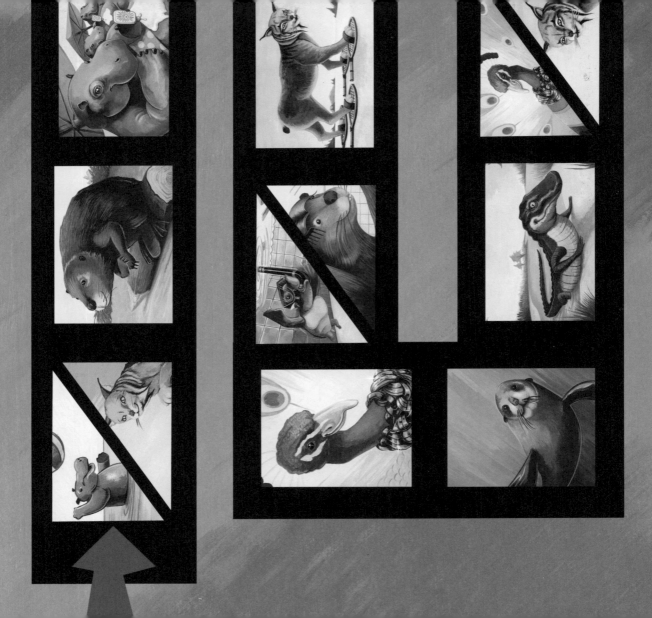